I0711294

ÉLÉPHANTE

Earth's Largest

Living Land

Animals

ÉLÉPHANTE INFORMATIONS

Elephants are mammals of the family Elephantidae and the largest existing land animals. Three species are currently recognised: the African bush elephant, the African forest elephant, and the Asian elephant. Elephantidae is the only surviving family of the order Proboscidea; extinct members include the mastodons.

ÉLÉPHANTE AFRICAN SAVANNA

However, in 2001 scientific data identified that African elephants are actually two different species, the African Savannah, (Loxodonta Africana) and the African forest (Loxodonta cyclotis), The primary differences with their physical confirmation is that the African forest elephant is more slender, slightly smaller with straighter, smaller tusk and their ears are more rounded. African savannah elephants are found in savannah zones in 37 countries south of the Sahara Desert.

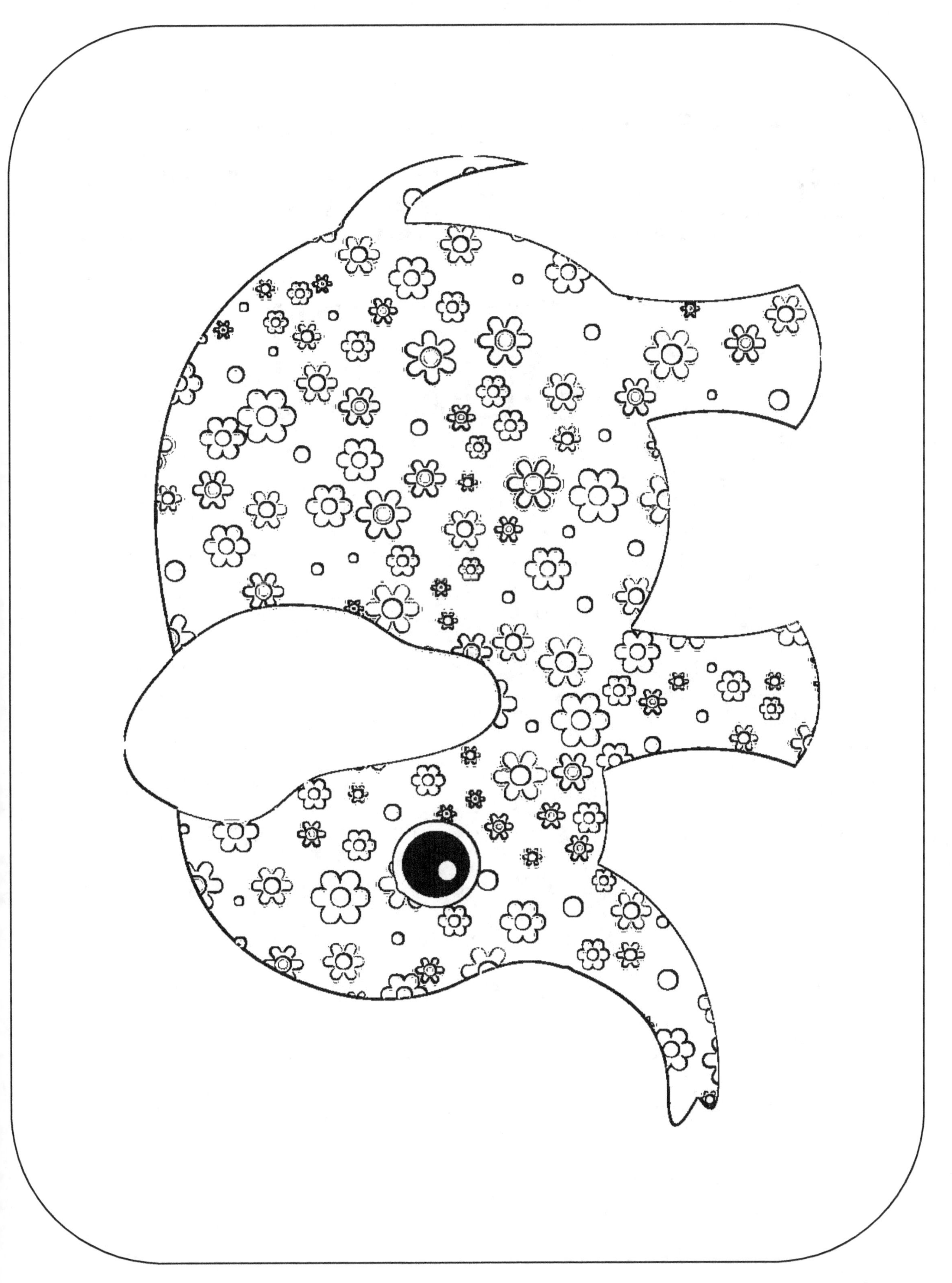

ÉLÉPHANTE ASIAN

The Asian elephant has four subspecies: Sri Lankan, Indian, Sumatran and Malaysian. Each of these sub species have slightly different characteristics, many are difficult to distinguish. Sri Lankan elephants tend to be slender with larger ears, and many Sri Lankan male elephants are tuskless. Indian elephants tend to be lighter-skinned, Sumatran elephants are slightly stockier and Malaysian elephants are a little smaller in stature. There are reports of pigmy elephants in Borneo but little is know about them due to the dense forest and inaccessible regions where they live. Elephants from Burma are not classified as a sub species but they tend to have a lot of hair and darker complexions.

ÉLÉPHANTE AFRICAN FOREST

African forest elephants
inhabit the dense
rainforests of west and
central Africa.

COMMUNICATION ÉLÉPHANTS

Communication is vital to elephants, who rely on a social network for survival. Although elephants can make a very wide range of sounds (10 octaves), they mostly communicate through low-frequency sounds called "rumbling."

COMMUNICATION ÉLÉPHANTS

Recent discoveries have shown that elephants can communicate over long distances by producing these sub-sonic rumblings which can travel through the ground faster than sound in air.

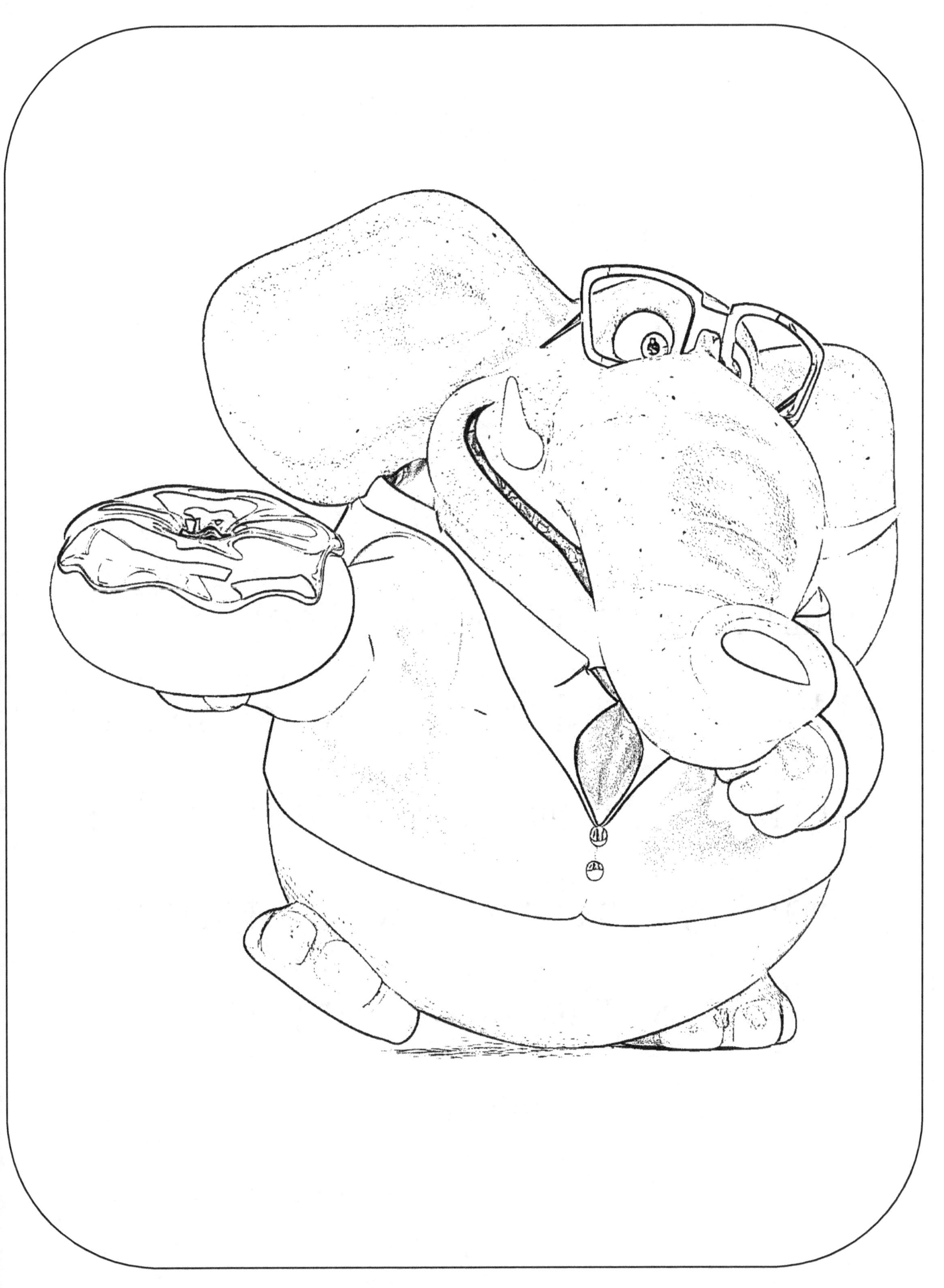

GENERAL CULTURAL INFORMATION ABOUT THE ELEPHANT

Males (bulls) leave their family groups when they reach puberty, and may live alone or with other males. Adult bulls mostly interact with family groups when looking for a mate.

GENERAL CULTURAL INFORMATION ABOUT THE ELEPHANT

African elephants are listed as vulnerable and Asian elephants as endangered by the International Union for Conservation of Nature (IUCN). One of the biggest threats to elephant populations is the ivory trade,

I LOVE YOU MOM

ÉLÉPHANTE MATING

Elephants are the only animals to have a temporal gland. When this gland becomes active the elephant enters a state of behaviour known as 'musth'. In the languages of northern India, musth (originally a Persian word) means a state of drunkenness, hilarity, ecstasy, desire or lust.

MATING

Musth is a condition unique to elephants, which has still not been scientifically explained. It affects sexually mature male elephants usually between the ages of 20 and 50.

INFANT MORTALITY IN CAPTIVE-BRED
ELEPHANTS

The infant-mortality rate for elephants in zoos is almost triple the rate in the wild. The overall infant-mortality rate for elephants in zoos is a staggering 40%

ELEPHANTS

INTELLIGENCE

Elephants are some of the most intelligent animals on Earth. Their brains weigh 11 lbs. (5 kg.), much more than the brain of any other land animal. Their brains have more complex folds than all animals except whales, which is thought to be a major factor in their intellect.

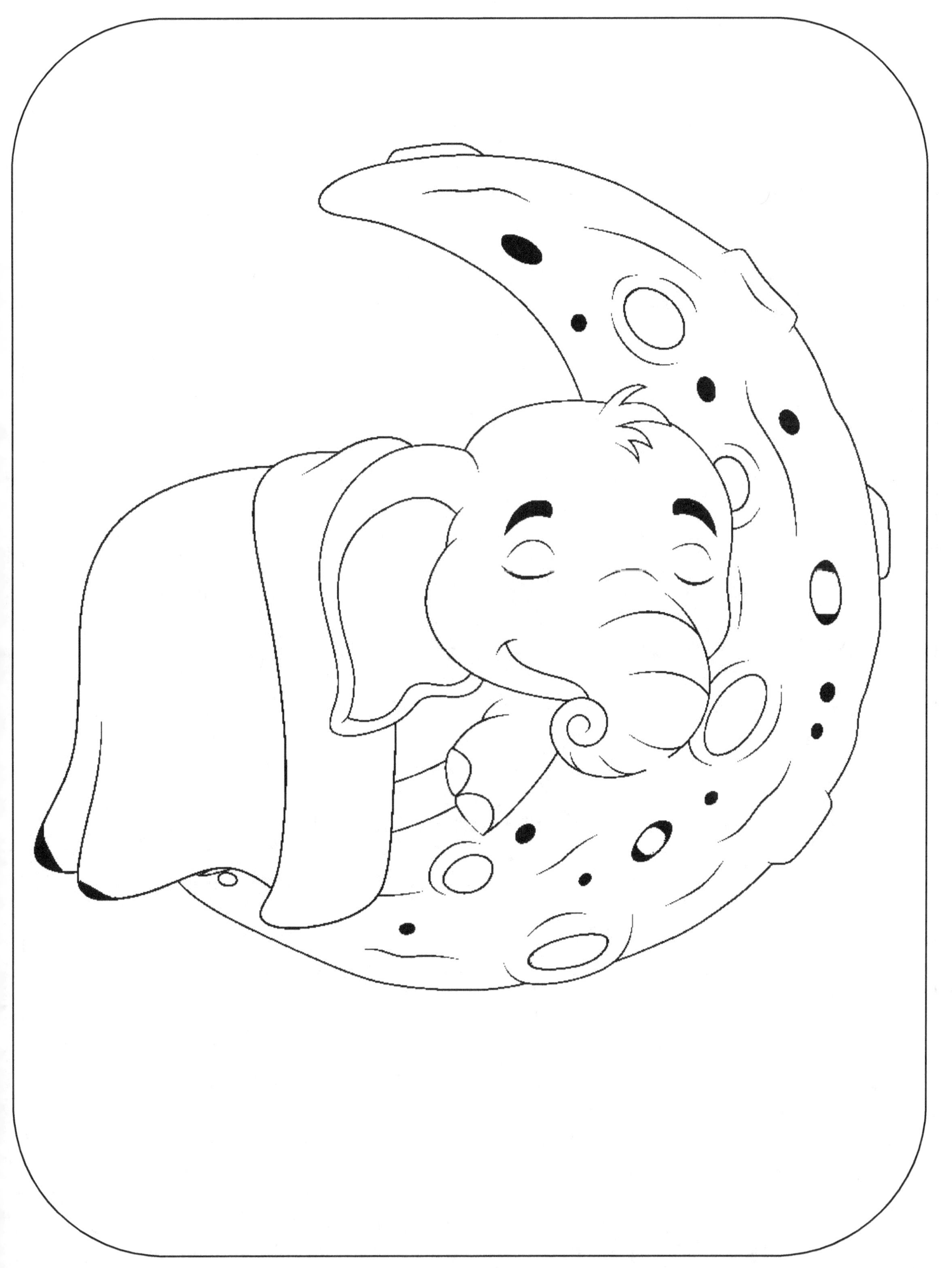

ELEPHANT

POPULATION IN THE WILD

The estimated numbers for elephants in the wild is 25,600 to 32,750 Asian elephants and 250,000-350,000 savanna elephants and 50,000-140,000 Forest elephants. Numbers from different studies vary, but the result is still the same, our elephants are disappearing from the wild.

ELEPHANT

POPULATION IN THE WILD

One study states African elephant population dropped by 50%, from 1.3 million to 600,000, between 1979 and 1989 because of poaching. About 8 elephants an hour (70,000/year) were poached during this period, until the CITES Ivory ban in 1989.

ELEPHANT POPULATION IN THE WILD

Another study published with 60 scientists in the journal PLOS One, who ran the largest study ever conducted in the central African forest, where elephants are being poached out of existence, has their own findings. Their study revealed 62% of forest elephants vanished from central Africa between 2002 and 2011.

ELEPHANT
POPULATION IN THE WILD

Asian elephants don't fair any better. It is estimated that the population has fallen by at least 50% over the last 60-75 years.

THE IMPACT OF A GROWING HUMAN POPULATION

The continually growing human population of tropical Asia has encroached upon the elephant's dense but dwindling forest habitat. About 20% of the world's human population lives in or near the present range of the Asian elephant

POACHING

Poaching of Asian elephants for ivory and meat remains a serious problem in many countries, especially in southern India (where 90% of the bulls are tuskers) and in north-east India where some people eat elephant meat.

POACHING

From 1995-1996, poaching of Asian elephants for hide, meat, and ivory increased sharply. The illegal trade in live elephants, ivory and hides across the Thai-Myanmar border has also become a serious conservation problem.

POACHING

A 1997 TRAFFIC report indicated that 7 years after international trade in ivory was banned, illegal commerce continued in the Far East, with South Korea and Taiwan being major markets.

ELEPHANTS
LIFE IN CAPTIVITY

The longevity of the life of elephants in the wild versus those in captivity is a highly argued subject.

National Geographic published an article in 2008, referencing a study done by British and Canadian scientist in 2002.

ELEPHANTS
LIFE IN CAPTIVITY

The data included elephants in European zoos (which house about half of the world's captive elephants), protected populations in Amboseli National Park in Kenya

THE IMPACT OF LIMITED SPACE

Many zoos are investing millions of dollars to slightly increase the size of their elephant exhibits, but elephants in captivity do not need a few additional square feet or even a couple of extra acres, they need a few additional square miles.

ELEPHANTS

ASSOCIATION WITH HUMANS

Working animal

Elephants have been working animals since at least the Indus Valley Civilization and continue to be used in modern times

ELÉPHANTS
IN THE WARFARE

Historically, elephants were considered formidable instruments of war. They were equipped with armour to protect their sides, and their tusks were given sharp points of iron or brass if they were large enough.

ELEPHANTES CULTURAL DEPICTIONS

In many cultures, elephants represent strength, power, wisdom, longevity, stamina, leadership, sociability, nurturance and loyalty.

Several cultural references emphasise the elephant's size and exotic uniqueness. For instance, a "white elephant" is a byword for something expensive, useless, and bizarre.

The expression "elephant in the room" refers to an obvious truth that is ignored or otherwise unaddressed.

ELEPHANTES CULTURAL DEPICTIONS

Elephants have been represented in art since Paleolithic times. Africa, in particular, contains many rock paintings and engravings of the animals, especially in the Sahara and southern Africa. In Asia, the animals are depicted as motifs in Hindu and Buddhist shrines and temples.

THREATS

The poaching of elephants for their ivory, meat and hides has been one of the major threats to their existence .

Historically, numerous cultures made ornaments and other works of art from elephant ivory, and its use rivalled that of gold. The ivory trade contributed to the African elephant population decline in the late 20th century.

This prompted international bans on ivory imports, starting with the United States in June 1989, and followed by bans in other North American countries, western European countries, and Japan.

Around the same time, Kenya destroyed all its ivory stocks.

ÉLÉPHANTE

In the past, they were used in war; today, they are often controversially put on display in zoos, or exploited for entertainment in circuses.

ELEPHANTS IN CIRCUS

Circus elephants not only face all of the emotional and physical issues that zoo elephants face but also a list of additional struggles. Circus elephants live a life being loaded into trucks and trains, carted from one city to the next, all in the name of 'entertainment'.

ELEPHANTS IN CIRCUS

These modes of transport are usually neither heated nor cooled, so they are exposed to whatever the temperatures of the cities they drive through provide.

ELEPHANTS IN CIRCUS

They are confined in these small, dark spaces for hours and sometimes days. They are then unloaded and kept in an area approximately the size of your living room. If they are lucky, they just wait there until it is time to perform, while others are taken away to walk in small circles, with numerous people on their back, for hours on end. They perform for the crowd, for five short minutes, and then the cycle starts all over again.

ELEPHANTS IN CIRCUS ATTACKS

Elephants can exhibit bouts of aggressive behaviour and engage in destructive actions against humans In Africa, groups of adolescent elephants damaged homes in villages after cullings in the 1970s and 1980s. Because of the timing, these attacks have been interpreted as vindictive

❑ All sources and references of information in the book with the rights to publish and share it with you to spread interest and culture

- https://en.wikipedia.org/wiki/Elephant#Association_with_humans

- https://www.livescience.com/27320-elephants.html#:~:text=Elephants%20are%20the%20largest%20land,animal%20with%20a%20similar%20physique.

- *Shoshani, J. (1998). "Understanding proboscidean evolution: a formidable task". Trends in Ecology and Evolution.* **13** *(12): 480–87.* doi:*10.1016/S0169-5347(98)01491-8. PMID 21238404.*